j391
E13c

Easterling, Lisa.
Clothing.

WITHDRAWN
MAR 17 2011

D0933558

Our Global Community

Clothing

Lisa Easterling

Heinemann Library
Chicago, Illinois

© 2007 Heinemann Library
a division of Reed Elsevier Inc.
Chicago, Illinois

Customer Service 888-454-2279
Visit our website at www.heinemannraintree.com

All rights reserved. No part of this publication may be reproduced or transmitted in any form or by any means, electronic or mechanical, including photocopying, recording, taping, or any information storage and retrieval system, without permission in writing from the publisher.

Designed by Joanna Hinton-Malivoire
Photo research by Ruth Smith
Printed and bound in China by South China Printing Co. Ltd.

11 10 09 08 07
10 9 8 7 6 5 4 3 2 1

The Library of Congress has cataloged the first edition of this book as follows:
Easterling, Lisa.
   Clothing / Lisa Easterling.
      p. cm. -- (Our global community)
   Includes bibliographical references and index.
   ISBN 978-1-4034-9405-4 (hc) -- ISBN 978-1-4034-9414-6 (pb) 1. Clothing and dress--Juvenile literature. I. Title.
   GT518.E37 2007
   391--dc22
                          2006034290

Acknowledgements
The publishers would like to thank the following for permission to reproduce photographs: Alamy pp. **9** (Blend Images), **15** (Around the World in a Viewfinder), **23** (Blend Images); Corbis pp. **4** (James Leynse), **5** (Michael Reynolds/epa), **6** (Galen Rowell), **8** (Fabio Cardoso/zefa), **10**, **11**, **12** (Jose Luis Pelaez, Inc.), **13** (Yang Liu), **16** (Penny Tweedie), **17** (Daniel Lainé), **18** (Peter Turnley), **19** (Roger Ressmeyer), **20** (Sergio Pitamitz), **23** (Yang Liu; Michael Reynolds/epa); Getty Images pp. **7** (Image Bank), **14** (Robert Harding).

Cover photograph reproduced with permission of Corbis/Peter Adams/zefa. Back cover photograph reproduced with permission of Alamy/Around the World in a Viewfinder.

Every effort has been made to contact copyright holders of any material reproduced in this book. Any omissions will be rectified in subsequent printings if notice is given to the publishers.

The paper used to print this books comes from sustainable resources.

Contents

Clothing

People wear clothing.

Clothing protects the body.

Types of Clothes

Clothes protect you from the cold.

Clothes protect you from sunshine.

Clothes are for work.

Some work clothes are uniforms.

Clothes are for sports.

Clothes are for outside.

Clothes are for special days.

Clothes are for holidays.

Clothing Around the World

Some people in Japan wear kimonos.

Kimonos are worn with wide belts.

kente cloth

Some people in Africa wear
kente cloth.

Kente cloth is worn for special times.

Some women in India wear saris.

sarong

Some men in Bali wear sarongs.

Clothing is different everywhere.

What kind of clothes do you wear?

What Is Clothing Made of?

- Clothing is made of cotton. Cotton comes from a plant.

- Clothing is made of wool. Wool comes from sheep.

- Clothing is made of silk. Silk comes from a silkworm.

- Clothing is made of linen. Linen comes from a plant.

Picture Glossary

 **holiday** a special day that happens on the same day every year

 **protect** to keep from harm

 **uniform** clothing that tells where you work

Index

Note to Parents and Teachers
This series expands children's horizons beyond their neighborhoods to show that communities around the world share similar features and rituals of daily life. The text has been chosen with the advice of a literacy expert to ensure that beginners can read the books independently or with moderate support. Stunning photographs visually support the text while engaging students with the material.

You can support children's nonfiction literacy skills by helping students use the table of contents, headings, picture glossary, and index.